What Can Animals Do?

By Meish Goldish

Scott Foresman
is an imprint of

Glenview, Illinois • Boston, Massachusetts • Chandler, Arizona •
Hoboken, New Jersey

Photographs

Every effort has been made to secure permission and provide appropriate credit for photographic material. The publisher deeply regrets any omission and pledges to correct errors called to its attention in subsequent editions.

Unless otherwise acknowledged, all photographs are the property of Pearson Education, Inc.

Photo locators denoted as follows: Top (T), Center (C), Bottom (B), Left (L), Right (R), Background (Bkgd)

Opener: Jupiter Images; **1** Strauss/Curtis/Corbis; **3** Jupiter Images; **4** imagebroker/Alamy Images; **5** Jupiter Images; **6** Jupiter Images; **7** ©Yahya Idiz/Fotolia; **8** Strauss/Curtis/Corbis.

ISBN 13: 978-0-328-46393-0
ISBN 10: 0-328-46393-0

10 11 12 13 14 V010 18 17 16 15 14

Eagles are special.
They can fly high.
They can fly fast.

Rescue dogs are special.
They can smell something
far away.
They can find missing people.

Sharks are special.

They can swim deep in the sea.

They can swim fast.

Cheetahs are special.
They have long, strong legs.
They are the fastest animals
on land.

Kangaroos are special.
They can hop high.
They can hop far.

Chameleons are special.
They start out as one color.
They can change to
another color.